KU-736-031

Philip Ardagh's Shortcuts

A FAST AND FUNNY GUIDE TO

Henry VIII

Philip Ardagh's Shortcuts

Elizabeth I
Florence Nightingale
Henry VIII
Julius Caesar
Marie Curie
Mary, Queen of Scots
Napoleon
Oliver Cromwell
Queen Victoria
William the Conqueror

Philip Ardagh's Shortcuts

A FAST AND FUNNY GUIDE TO

Henry VIII

Illustrated by Alan Rowe

MACMILLAN CHILDREN'S BOOKS

This one's for my editor, Gaby Morgan,
for being nice to big men with beards!

First published 1999 by Macmillan Children's Books

This edition published 2013 by Macmillan Children's Books
a division of Macmillan Publishers Limited
20 New Wharf Road, London N1 9RR
Basingstoke and Oxford
Associated companies throughout the world
www.panmacmillan.com

ISBN 978-1-4472-4029-7

Text copyright © Philip Ardagh 1999
Illustrations copyright © Alan Rowe 1999

The right of Philip Ardagh and Alan Rowe to be identified as the
author and illustrator of this work has been asserted by them in
accordance with the Copyright, Designs and Patents Act 1988.

All rights reserved. No part of this publication may be
reproduced, stored in or introduced into a retrieval system, or
transmitted, in any form or by any means (electronic, mechanical,
photocopying, recording or otherwise), without the prior written
permission of the publisher. Any person who does any unauthorized
act in relation to this publication may be liable to criminal
prosecution and civil claims for damages.

1 3 5 7 9 8 6 4 2

A CIP catalogue record for this book is available from the British Library.

Printed and bound by CPI Group (UK) Ltd, Croydon CR0 4YY

This book is sold subject to the condition that it shall not,
by way of trade or otherwise, be lent, resold, hired out,
or otherwise circulated without the publisher's prior consent
in any form of binding or cover other than that in which
it is published and without a similar condition including this
condition being imposed on the subsequent purchaser.

CONTENTS

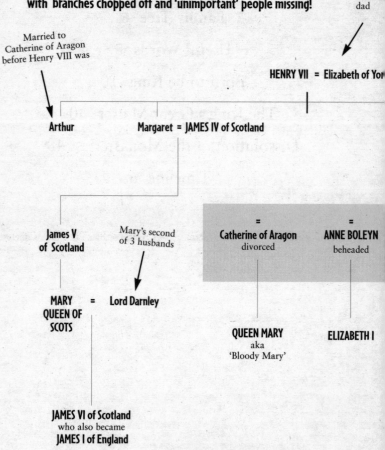

The Author's Hacked About
FAMILY TREE OF
HENRY VIII
with branches chopped off and 'unimportant' people missing!

Henry's mum and dad

Married to
Catherine of Aragon
before Henry VIII was

HENRY VII = Elizabeth of York

Arthur   **Margaret** = **JAMES IV of Scotland**

**James V
of Scotland**

Mary's second
of 3 husbands

=
Catherine of Aragon
divorced

=
ANNE BOLEYN
beheaded

**MARY
QUEEN OF
SCOTS**   =   **Lord Darnley**

QUEEN MARY
aka
'Bloody Mary'

ELIZABETH I

JAMES VI of Scotland
who also became
JAMES I of England

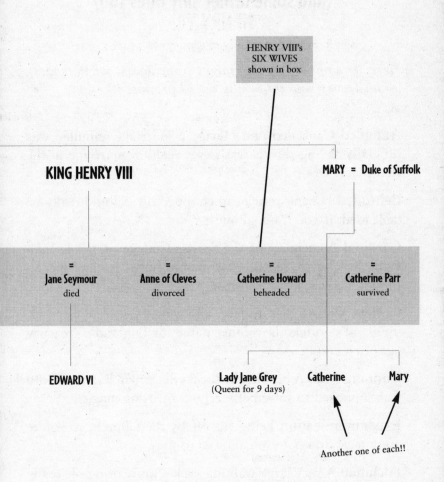

HENRY VIII's
SIX WIVES
shown in box

KING HENRY VIII   MARY = Duke of Suffolk

=   =   =   =
Jane Seymour   Anne of Cleves   Catherine Howard   Catherine Parr
died   divorced   beheaded   survived

EDWARD VI   Lady Jane Grey   Catherine   Mary
                                  (Queen for 9 days)

Another one of each!!

USEFUL WORDS
(and some rather silly ones too)

Here are some words you might come across when reading about Henry, and those silly ones I promised!

Annulled Cancelled out. Having a marriage annulled was officially saying that it was never really a marriage in the first place. Ooops!

Beheaded Having your head chopped off. Should really be deheaded, if you think about it.

Cardinal A member of the Sacred College of the Roman Catholic Church, second only in importance to the Pope. So there!

Coffers Chests that money and valuables were kept in. 'England's coffers' is another name for England's Treasury . . . often empty.

Cunning Man A bit like the local village witch doctor, who was supposed to solve petty crimes by using magic!

Excommunication Being cut off by the Church, so you're an outcast and not even allowed to pray.

Filchman A very large walking stick – more of a pole really – and ideal for hitting people with.

Heresy An opinion that's different to the view of the official Church.

Tyburn A place in London where executions took place. Most victims were hanged – people are 'hanged', pictures are 'hung' – but some of the more important ones (people, not pictures) were beheaded instead.

BORN TO BE KING

Henry VIII's family name was Tudor. The 'VIII' bit is just Latin for 'eight' – a five (V) and three ones (III). The number eight simply tells us that there were seven other King Henrys on the English throne sometime before him. Henry's dad (Henry VII), for example, was King of England, but his grandfather wasn't. So how did the Tudor family end up with the English crown?

OWE IT TO OWEN

Back in 1415, the King of England was another man called Henry – Henry V this time, but certainly not a Tudor. Henry V is famous for leading the English army into battle that year, against the French at a place called Agincourt. Fighting for the English was a Welshman called Owen Tudor. (That last name sound familiar now, does it?) The English army of 5,700 defeated the French army of 25,000. Henry V then married a French princess called Catherine of Valois and they had a son. When the boy was just nine months old, Henry V died and the boy became king.

ANOTHER HENRY!

With her son Henry VI (the sixth) officially on the throne, Catherine heard rumours that a clerk of the wardrobe – that was a job title, not a piece of furniture – was secretly dating one of her ladies-in-waiting at the court. This was very naughty and certainly not allowed, so she went to confront him ... but ended up marrying him instead. The man's name? Why, Owen Tudor, of course! This caused BIG TROUBLE. Catherine should have got permission before doing something like that, so those ruling on behalf of the young king sent Catherine to a convent and threw Owen Tudor into Newgate Jail. He managed to escape twice and was recaptured twice.

BOUNCING BABIES

This didn't stop Catherine and Owen from having four children, though. And those children had 'royal blood' in them. After all, Catherine was the mother of King Henry VI, wasn't she, and had even been queen herself. Their dad, Owen Tudor, meanwhile, was pardoned, released from jail and became a royal park keeper back in Wales! Fifty years later – after winning the Wars of the Roses – Owen Tudor's grandson (our Henry VIII's dad) was able to claim the crown of England (as Henry VII) as his prize and Henry VIII followed him. All thanks to Owen Tudor, ex-soldier, ex-prisoner and park keeper.

THE WARS OF THE ROSES

This war was between two great 'houses' of England. Not the bricks-and-mortar kind of houses, but important families and their supporters. On one side were the Yorks, with their emblem of the white rose, and on the other were the Lancastrians, with their red rose emblem. Henry VIII's father, Henry VII, was a Tudor from the House of Lancaster. When he became king, he married Elizabeth of York and created the emblem of the Tudor rose – both red and white. So, in a way, both the Lancastrians *and* the Yorks won!

IT'S A BOY!

Henry VIII – who I'll call just plain 'Henry' from now on (but will give all the other Henrys their numbers or titles) – was born on 28 June 1491 at Greenwich Palace. He had a big brother called Arthur, who was Prince of Wales and the heir to the throne. Henry's title (apart from being a prince) was Duke of York. When, in 1502, Arthur died Henry was suddenly next in line to be king.

AN EDUCATION

Because Henry was a prince, it meant that he didn't have to go to school. (Hoorah!) But it didn't mean that he got out of having lessons. (Boo! Hiss!) He had his own private tutor called John Skelton. Skelton was a priest and a poet and always wore black robes. Unusually for teachers in those days, he didn't beat Henry much. Sometimes, a nobleman named Lord Mountjoy helped teach Henry too. Henry learnt everything from French and Latin to warfare, chess, dancing and card playing! There were very few books around, because printing had only just been invented.

SUPER DAD

Henry's dad, Henry VII, was a very good king. Uniting the houses of York and Lancaster had been a clever move when he'd married Elizabeth of York, and he did plenty of other smart things too. He made the powerful families of England less powerful, taking away their right to have huge private armies of their own. The only army in England should be the *king's* army, which made peace a much more likely prospect. Henry's dad also did a lot for law and order for ordinary people, creating justices of the peace and (less popular) official tax collectors.

THE YOUNG KING

Following his father's death on 21 April 1509, Henry became 'Henry VIII', aged just seventeen. Today most people think of Henry VIII as being fat and bearded, but it's important to remember that, when he first became king, he was slim, dashing and even thought to be good-looking. In fact, some people compared him to Alexander the Great!

HENRY'S FIRST QUEEN

Between becoming king and being crowned at his coronation, Henry married his long-time sweetheart and fiancée, Catherine of Aragon. This was just the sort of smart thing his father would have done. Catherine was the daughter of the King of Spain, and Spain was a very powerful country. This match would be good for England. Catherine of Aragon had been married to Henry's brother Arthur. When Arthur

died, she'd become engaged to Henry . . . even though he was only twelve at the time! Now he was older, they got married less than two weeks before the coronation. This way Henry's bride could be crowned queen at the same time that he was crowned king.

CROWNING THE NEW KING

Henry was crowned on 23 June 1509. Rising at 6.00 a.m., he had a bath (which was extremely unusual), went to mass, then dressed in his finest clothes which included a crimson shirt and jacket of finest satin, covered with a fur-edged coat, also bright crimson. On his head was a little cap, later swapped for the crown. The coronation took place at Westminster Abbey and everyone wore fabulous robes and dresses. It was the brightest, best and richest-looking public spectacle the country had seen.

FUN, FUN, FUN

Now that Henry was king, he wanted life at the royal court to be fun, fun, fun. He loved his wife – kings often married for reasons other than love, remember – and he loved food, drink, gambling, singing and dancing and a whole host of other things. His father might have been a good king, but Henry thought him pretty B-O-R-I-N-G. Henry and Catherine moved from palace to palace (that's Greenwich, Richmond, Westminster and Windsor, not forgetting the Tower of London) having party after party!

BEHIND THE SCENES

Such serious partying needed a great deal of organization, and that was down to Henry's Lord Steward. Steward wasn't a name, but a title. A steward was in charge of all the eating arrangements and, for Henry's Lord Steward, that could mean banquets for 1,000 guests. Luckily for the Lord Steward, he had a staff of about five hundred men, women and children to help. (Queen Catherine, alone, had about 160 people looking after her!)

NOT SUCH FUN FOR SOME

Life wasn't one non-stop party for all Henry's officials and courtiers, though. Starting as he meant to go on, he had Edmund Dudley and Sir Richard Empson beheaded. (Yup, off with their heads!) They'd been his father's taxmen and no one liked paying tax much, so Henry knew that this would be a very popular move. Of course, he could simply have taken their jobs away from them, but this was much more fun!

HOW THE OTHER HALF LIVED

It was during Henry's reign that people began to build grand houses out of brick. Before that, the grandest houses had been built from stone, and before that, timber, wattle and daub (sticks, plaster and animal dung). If Henry visited a house and really liked it, he would persuade the owner to present it to him as a gift. It didn't take much persuasion because you couldn't really refuse a king . . . especially a king who'd already beheaded a few people. The most famous building he acquired that way was Hampton Court, from a man named Thomas Wolsey.

A MAN CALLED WOLSEY

Henry wasn't really interested in details. He wanted things done, but he happily left someone else to do the actual doing. At the start of his reign, that someone was a man named Cardinal Thomas Wolsey. As Lord Chancellor, Wolsey took care of the day-to-day details of government, which made him very powerful indeed. Wolsey's big failing was that he liked to show off as much as Henry himself, which was a very dangerous thing to do. Like the king, Wolsey loved money and possessions and dressing in fine clothes. He even wanted to be Pope – the head of the whole

17

Roman Catholic Church and one of the most important people in the western world!

THE MAN IN RED

Cardinals often wore red at official functions – it was a bit like a uniform – but Thomas Wolsey liked to wear red all the time, including a cap on his head. Of course, there were different shades of red to choose from, and he liked scarlet or crimson . . . made of the very finest of satin, which he could well afford. This probably clashed a bit with the orange he often carried around with him. Yes, orange as in the *fruit* . . . though it wasn't always the same orange. It was filled with vinegar and herbs and God-knows-what, and was supposed to hide the nasty smells of everyday life in Henry's time. (Wolsey would give it a jolly good sniff when out and about amongst common people!)

SHOW OFF TO THE WORLD

Henry was eager to show the world that England was an important country and that he was an important king. He wanted to find an impressive way of showing off the country's wealth and importance to others. In 1520, a tournament was arranged on the continent, near Calais (which was English-owned). There were splendid tents and one was made of golden cloth, giving the event its name: *The Field of the Cloth of Gold.*

THE FIELD OF THE CLOTH OF GOLD

Over 5,000 people sailed over from England for the month-long tournament of free wine and entertainment. (There were fountains of wine. Literally.) The highlight of the tournament was supposed to be the meeting between Henry and Francis I, King of France, on 7 June 1520. They both pretended that the event was designed to create an important understanding between their two countries. It was really an excuse to see who could be the most extravagant and stylish - the show-offs!

NO FIGHTING PLEASE

Tournaments included jousts between knights and noblemen, but it was agreed that the two kings would not fight, just meet. And meet they did, both dressed in the latest stunning fashions. Henry wore gold and silver – and so did his horse, to match! Two weeks of English and French festivities followed, with plenty of singing and dancing. Despite the 'no fighting' agreement, Henry then went and spoilt everything by insisting on a quick wrestle . . . which he promptly lost! In next to no time, the loyal English were accusing Francis I of cheating (for how else could a Frenchman have won?) and things turned a little sour.

SECRET TALKS

The truth be told, Henry wasn't a great fan of the French king anyway. Part way through the month-long tournament, he'd snuck back over to England and met up with Emperor Charles V, Catherine of Aragon's nephew. Charles V was ruler of the Holy Roman Empire. I'm certainly not the first person to point this out – and I certainly won't be the last – but it's worth making it clear that the Holy Roman Empire wasn't holy, wasn't Roman and wasn't even really an empire. It was a group of small, squabbling German states, but 'Holy Roman Empire' sounded good. Talking of good, Charles V was also now King of Spain, for good measure, and *hated* Francis I of France. He and Henry signed a treaty 'of common cause' against the French. By 1522, England and France were at war once more.

A VICTORY . . . OF SORTS

Siding with Charles V seemed a smart move. In 1525, the forces of the Holy Roman Empire not only defeated the French at Pavia but also captured King Francis of France himself! Wolsey was quick to take advantage of the situation, and proposed that Henry march his army into Paris . . . an idea which Charles was less than thrilled by. It was mainly the Holy Roman Empire's money and soldiers that had been poured into the war, and Charles wasn't about to hand over French lands to Henry for his limited help!

FABULOUS FORCES

England then switched sides. It was Wolsey's idea, of course, because he was eager to be all-powerful in Europe. If Charles wasn't happy about Henry and England keeping Paris, he argued, then Henry should simply become his enemy! The head of the Roman Catholic Church was Pope Clement VII, and Wolsey was one of his cardinals. (Don't forget that England was a Roman Catholic country at the time.) Wolsey met with the Pope and others who

were fed up with Charles having so much power. They hatched a plot against the Holy Roman Empire. When Francis of France was released in 1526, he too joined the plot. For the first time in ages, England and France were on the *same* side. (GASP!)

A BAD MOVE

Charles V was no pushover, despite his powerful enemies. In May 1527, his troops ran amok in Rome, and even though no one would dare officially take Pope Clement VII prisoner, that's pretty much what he became. In 1529, the French hurriedly made peace with Charles, having suffered yet more defeats. Fortunately for them, Charles didn't occupy France, because he now had control over most of continental Europe. Much to Wolsey's embarrassment, England was ignored ... It obviously wasn't worth the effort to invade!

A RUDE AWAKENING

It must have been about then that Henry realized the terrible truth (shudder). His man Wolsey had led him to believe that England was a very important player on the European stage. (In other words, if events in Europe were in a play, England – and Henry – would get one of the biggest parts, with the best lines and some good action sequences.) It now turned out that Europe – and the likes of Charles V – could do what they liked without him ... (In this version of the play, Henry might be off-stage doing the catering.) And all Wolsey's time and effort (and England's coffers) being spent wheeling and dealing in European matters had another effect. Things had been left to go wrong at home.

GREAT HARRY

At the start of his reign, Henry had known that it wouldn't be long before England and France were at war again. It was traditional. They always seemed to be fighting each other. Perhaps it was because they were only separated by the Channel, so France was just a short ship's ride away ... Anyway, Henry wanted to strengthen the English army and be prepared. At the same time, he wanted to build a bigger, better navy. Not him personally, of course. Wolsey did a lot of the organizing. Henry's new navy had some super-sized ships in it. The biggest, called *Great Harry*, could carry 260 sailors and 400 soldiers, and weighed 1,000 tons. But this cost money ... Money which was not being spent on matters close to home.

THE MARY ROSE

Henry's most famous ship was the Mary Rose, but it's famous for the wrong reason. It sank! In 1545, the French were planning to invade England – surprise, surprise – and their ships appeared off the coast near Portsmouth. The massive Mary Rose sailed out to meet the enemy, which turned and ran (or whatever it is that ships do). Turning to sail triumphantly back to harbour, the Mary Rose capsized, drowning almost 500 men. Despite Henry's efforts, the ship lay at the bottom of the sea for over 430 years, until parts of it were salvaged in 1982.

A COSTLY BUSINESS

War was expensive, and not just in the loss of human lives (which wasn't Henry's main worry anyway). Records show that, between Henry coming to the throne in 1509 and the date of 12 June 1513, the Treasury had paid out over one million pounds . . . and that didn't all go on partying. Far from it, in fact. Nearly 70 per cent of it was spent on war . . . nearly half of which was spent *in one week*, in preparation to fight the French! More money was needed and, in 1523, Wolsey tried to raise this with his 'Amicable Grant'.

THE NOT-SO-AMICABLE GRANT

'Amicable' means friendly, but there was nothing friendly about the Amicable Grant – which wasn't really a grant either, it was a tax. All in all, it might have been a teeny-weeny bit more honest for Wolsey to have called it the Unpopular Tax, because that's what it was. If you owned property, you paid the tax to help pay for the war. There was uproar. People just didn't want to pay. Many people couldn't afford to anyway, and it looked like things were about to turn very nasty. With reports of possible armed rebellion in Kent and East Anglia, Henry cancelled the Amicable Grant saying that he'd never authorized it. Not only that, he automatically pardoned anyone who'd refused to pay Wolsey . . . which was more than a public humiliation for the cardinal. It was also a reminder to Wolsey of who was really boss.

GONE TO HIS HEAD?

Wolsey certainly liked power. He's famous for starting out by issuing orders which began with 'the King says', later changing that to 'we say' and, finally, 'I say'. The power had gone to his head. He'd done rather well for himself from being a butcher's (and a Mrs Butcher's) son to a cardinal to Lord Chancellor, too. He was also very rich. Rumours spread that he'd used the king's money to build up his own personal fortune. In fact, he'd used money from the Church . . . and matters of the Church were to be his downfall.

A MARRIAGE ON THE ROCKS

Sad to say, but Henry didn't love his wife any more. Catherine of Aragon was five years older than him, approaching forty (which seemed a lot older in those days than it does now, because people died much younger then), and getting a bit dumpy and wrinkled. Now, there's nothing wrong with being dumpy or wrinkled, or both for that matter, except that Henry didn't like it. To make matters worse, Catherine had 'failed' to give him a healthy son.

THE TRAGEDY OF CATHERINE'S CHILDREN

Henry and Catherine of Aragon's first child, a daughter, was stillborn. Their next three children were either sickly and died, or were stillborn. Finally, poor Catherine gave birth to a healthy child on 18 February 1516. Henry had her

christened Mary after his favourite sister. (She later earned the name 'Bloody Mary', but I'll save the reason why for another time.)

GOOD GOD!

Despite all the fun partying, Henry and Catherine were enthusiastic Catholics. But, after ten years on the throne of England and much praying and promises to God, there was no male heir – no prince to become king should Henry die. Then Henry had been naughty-naughty and had an affair with one of Catherine's ladies-in-waiting, by the name of Elizabeth Blount. They saw a lot of each other and, in 1519, had a healthy bouncing baby boy. In Henry's mind, that proved that the lack of sons in his marriage to Catherine was his *wife's* 'fault', not his!

A GOOD CATHOLIC . . . SOMETIMES

In Germany, a man named Martin Luther had broken away from the Catholic faith and was preaching what was seen as heresy – against the teachings of the Church. He published a book full of his ideas in 1520. In 1521, a book appeared in London called 'The Defence of the Seven Sacraments' which argued for the Church and against Luther. It was a best-seller all over Europe . . . and Henry had written it! He even dedicated it to the Pope. In recognition of this, on 11 October 1521, the Pope gave Henry the title 'Defender of the Faith'. Despite everything that was to follow (and, boy, was there lots to follow), Henry was proud of the title until the day he died.

ANNE BOLEYN

Elizabeth Blount was no longer at the royal court and Henry had a new mistress called Mary Boleyn. Mary had a great deal of influence over the king and persuaded him to make her younger sister, Anne, one of the queen's ladies-in-waiting. Anne Boleyn's eyes are said to have been 'black and beautiful', and she had *six* fingers on one hand. She also had a number of admirers, including the poet Sir Thomas Wyatt and Henry Percy, son of the Earl of Northumberland. Anne obviously liked Percy and might have married him . . . except for Cardinal Wolsey sticking his nose in and putting an end to it. This was probably on Henry's instructions.

DO THE RIGHT THING!

It soon became clear that Henry was more interested in Anne than Mary Boleyn, but the king was in for a shock. When he made his royal advances towards her, she made it clear that she had no wish to be a royal mistress, but would happily be his wife! She then left the royal court and went back to her family home at Hever Castle in Kent . . . This was a smart move because a great way of making Henry want something even more was to say that he couldn't have it. He was KING, wasn't he? He bombarded her with love letters.

THE ILLEGITIMATE HEIR

Henry loved the son he'd had by Elizabeth Blount. He had christened him Henry Fitzroy after himself and, when the boy was six, made him Duke of Richmond. There was even talk of finding him a foreign princess to marry and it was

made clear that, if Henry had no legitimate son, this boy would become king after him. Even Catherine agreed to this in public. Amazingly, Pope Clement VII was even prepared to let Henry Fitzroy marry Henry and Catherine's daughter – his own half-sister – to cement his right to England's crown!!! But Henry still wanted a legitimate heir, to be sure that no one could dispute the Tudors' right to sit on the throne of England for many generations ... and Anne Boleyn wanted to marry Henry, so the choice seemed simple. Henry must divorce Catherine, marry Anne, and he and his new wife would have a son.

THE KING'S GREAT MATTER

Henry gave Cardinal Wolsey the job of getting an official annulment of the marriage between him and Catherine of Aragon. The Roman Catholic Church doesn't allow divorce, but does allow annulments under very special circumstances. As a cardinal of Rome, Wolsey set up a secret tribunal to 'charge' Henry with being unlawfully married to Catherine. The excuse they dreamt up for the marriage being 'unlawful' was that Henry had married his brother's wife . . . the fact that his brother was *dead* didn't come into it. Catherine wasn't aware of the tribunal and neither was the Pope, but Wolsey intended to annul the marriage then convince him to agree to it. The whole thing was a fudge! Then the Pope was more or less kidnapped by Catherine's nephew Charles V, which I mentioned back on page 22, and the whole thing had to be dropped.

But you can't take me prisoner. I'm Pope!

Prisoner, Your Holiness? I'm simply trying to cure your bad back!

THE CRAFTY CARDINAL

Now Thomas Wolsey switched to Plan B. He would try to convince the Pope that, as long as he was being held by Charles V, he should pass his authority on to someone else . . . and that this 'acting pope' should be none other than himself: Cardinal Wolsey! Unfortunately for the cardinal, on 22 June 1527, Henry made the mistake of telling Catherine of Aragon that he thought that they hadn't been properly married for the past eighteen years! Wolsey had expected the king not to say anything until the marriage had been successfully annulled. Now the secret was out, and Catherine sent a message to her nephew Charles V.

A VERY PUBLIC PROBLEM

Suddenly, Henry's private wedding difficulties were the talk of Europe. Not only that, Charles V wrote to Aunt Catherine offering her his full support as well as informing Clement VII (his prisoner, the Pope) that he should consider removing Wolsey's powers. Henry himself was getting fed up with Wolsey, particularly because the cardinal seemed to think that Henry's next wife should be a French noblewoman called Renée . . . He didn't think Anne Boleyn was suitable!

THE CARDINAL COCKS UP

While Cardinal Wolsey was in Europe in 1527, trying to whip up support for him to be made 'acting pope', Henry asked the Pope directly if he would not only annul his marriage to poor old Catherine, but also give the thumbs-up to him marrying Anne Boleyn. When Wolsey returned to England, he found the king a changed man.

Suddenly, Henry *liked* doing things for himself. In the past, he'd signed any letter Wolsey put in front of him without even bothering to read it. Not any more. Not only that, Wolsey was only allowed to see Henry when Anne Boleyn agreed to it!

BACK IN FAVOUR

Henry's approaches to Pope Clement VII were a complete flop. Wolsey, however, had an unexpected success. The Pope suddenly agreed to let the whole affair be sorted out in England by another cardinal called Lorenzo Campeggio. Once a friend of Henry's, as well as being a cardinal Campeggio was also Bishop of Salisbury. Matters should soon be sorted out, so long as everyone survived the plague . . .

THE PLAGUE

In 1528, the 'sweating sickness' was particularly bad in England, and London was one of the easiest places to catch it. Henry was convinced that he'd get it so fled London and kept on the move. He attended at least three masses a day, wrote several wills and kept trying all the quack medicines that were supposed to protect one. He'd left Anne Boleyn in court . . . and she hadn't been looking too well when he'd fled. What a caring guy!

ILLNESS AND ACCIDENTS

Henry had many illnesses and accidents in his life. In 1514 he'd had smallpox (which was often a killer). In 1521, he caught malaria from a mosquito bite. In 1524 he forgot to put his visor down in a friendly joust and got bits of shattered lance in his face. In 1525, when out hawking, he tried to polevault across a ditch . . . but he was too heavy for the pole which snapped. He landed head-first in the mud with such force that his head got stuck and he couldn't breath. He had to be rescued by a footman. Then, in 1528, an ulcer appeared on one of his legs, soon to be followed by many more on both of them. In the end, Henry was unable to walk at all. To top it all, he used to get horrible headaches!

TROUBLEMAKER

What our Henry had no way of knowing was that Cardinal Campeggio was on a mission of time-wasting! It usually took about six weeks to travel from Rome to England. This may sound a long time, but Campeggio took *four months*. Once he'd arrived, things got even worse. Instead of looking into the annulment, he announced that it was his duty to try to repair Henry and Catherine's broken marriage! Campeggio's special tribunal didn't open until 18 June 1529. That was eight months after he'd first arrived in London.

FROM BAD TO WORSE

If Henry had thought that, now the tribunal had opened, things might begin to go in his favour, he was sadly (and badly) mistaken! Catherine appeared in person and, kneeling at the king's feet, sobbed, 'For the love of God, let me have justice and right.' She then confronted Henry, saying that if he could prove she'd done anything unlawful, she was 'content to depart to my great shame and dishonour'. She then left the Blackfriars court. Henry was gobsmacked. Just over a month later, Campeggio adjourned the court until October!

WOLSEY LOSES OUT

Now everything was a complete and utter public mess and Henry blamed Cardinal Wolsey. Hadn't he been supposed to sort the matter out swiftly and secretly ages ago? Now Wolsey found that his usual rooms at court were occupied by someone else. He found that the king would rather go riding with Anne Boleyn than discuss important matters with him. On 22 September 1529, he was ordered to surrender the Lord Chancellor's great seal. (He was Lord Chancellor, so this was a bit like a cop being asked to hand in his badge.) Wolsey refused until he saw the king's handwriting on the order. He is said to have broken down and cried.

ESCAPING THE BLOCK

Henry wanted more than Wolsey's job off him, he wanted his life. The king was angry and, if he wasn't going to get his own way, at least Wolsey would pay for it. Wolsey would be tried, though everyone knew how that trial would end: at the executioner's block with Wolsey's severed head in a basket. But Henry was denied that. On 29 November 1530, Wolsey died in Leicester on the way to the trial. He was pompous to the end, saying that if he'd served God as well as he'd served Henry, God wouldn't have given him grey hairs!

LIFE AFTER WOLSEY

With Thomas Wolsey out of the way, Henry needed another Lord Chancellor and he wasn't about to choose another churchman. Instead, he chose another Thomas – Thomas More, this time. More was a lawyer, not a cardinal, and Henry had known him for years. Thomas More is famous for being called 'a man for all seasons'. In other words, he could be happy and funny, or serious and sad . . . whatever was required of him. Unfortunately, he didn't always see eye to eye with his king.

JUST SAY 'NO'? NO

When Henry first offered Thomas More the job of Lord Chancellor, he said 'no'. He was a devout Roman Catholic and believed that Henry and Catherine of Aragon should stay married. But Henry wouldn't take 'no' for an answer. He said that More *must* take the job, but that he'd never be forced to do anything against his religious beliefs. The plans for divorce or annulment would be dealt with by other people. Thomas accepted the job.

ANY MORE, SIR THOMAS?

Historians with time on their hands before lunch sometimes divide Henry VIII's advisers into 'doers' and 'thinkers'. Wolsey was certainly a 'doer' and Sir Thomas More a 'thinker' . . . but More did some 'doing' too. In fact, he took part in drawing up forty-four articles listing all the terrible things Cardinal Wolsey was supposed to have done. He also found time to write books, including a couple on heresy, which is any opinion which differs from the view of the official Church. Of course, the official Church in England was still the Catholic Church. When that changed, More's views on heresy proved far less popular, even dangerous ... for him.

YET ANOTHER THOMAS

When it came to sorting out the mess with Catherine of Aragon, Henry called in yet *another* Thomas – and, yes, that does make things confusing. This Thomas was one Thomas Cromwell. His father was a blacksmith, but making horseshoes didn't interest Thomas. He left his father to it and went to Italy as a 'soldier of fortune' – pay him enough and he'd fight on your side. Later, he became a merchant and a lawyer. In 1520 he'd become a member of Wolsey's household, when Wolsey was possibly the most powerful man in England. He became a member of parliament in 1529, was a member of the Privy Council in 1531 and was a well-respected royal adviser. If this speedy rise in importance made him happy, it didn't show. He always looks gloomy in his portraits!

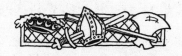

THE OTHER OTHER THOMAS

Another important Thomas in Henry's life was the churchman Thomas Cranmer. You'll find his name cropping up right to the very end. He was ordained a Roman Catholic priest in 1523, and in 1529 suggested that the question of Henry's marriage (or divorce) be looked at by the universities of Europe. Because this was a neat way of stopping the matter being left solely to the all-powerful Pope, Henry liked it. He liked Cranmer too.

CHANGING TACTICS

When Cardinal Campeggio announced that the whole marriage problem would have to be dealt with back in Rome, Henry decided that enough was enough. He was too proud a man to go and beg his cause to the Pope in person . . . that would be on foreign soil. Here, in England, he was in charge. With Thomas Wolsey gone and Thomas More not involved, Henry took matters into his own hands. He would turn his subjects – the people of England – against the Church.

A STATE WITHIN A STATE

Like most Roman Catholic countries in Europe, much of England's land actually belonged to the Roman Catholic Church and so to Rome. A third of it did . . . which was more than Henry himself owned! Many churchmen abused their power and wealth (as did many non-churchmen, of course), and some bishops earned more than England's top noblemen. (Noble*women* didn't earn anything. That was the way of the world back then.) As a result, many people – rich and poor – hated the Church, and Henry was about to use that hate to *his* advantage.

ABOVE THE LAW

What made the Church really unpopular were the tithes. These were taxes ordinary people had to pay to the Church for a whole variety of things. Tithes were based on a proportion of a person's income so even the very, very poor had to pay something. There were special Church courts that made sure you paid, or suffered if you didn't. They had nothing to do with the ordinary law of the land, and you couldn't appeal against a sentence. If that wasn't bad enough, if a clergyman (churchman) was accused of breaking the law, he could demand the right to be tried in a Church court instead of an ordinary one. Because he was tried by his friends and colleagues, more often than not he'd be found innocent!

ACTION AT LAST

Henry let it be known that he'd sort out the Church in England, getting rid of all the corruption and greed. This wasn't really his job – it was the Pope's – but he had parliament on his side. In 1529, pleased with their king's new approach, they sent him a petition. In it, they asked Henry to explain what 'laws of God' allowed churchmen to be greedy, have many jobs, buy and sell goods and live miles

away from the parishes of the people they were supposed to be caring for. A number of bishops had seats in the House of Lords. When they heard about the petition, it's said that they 'frowned and grunted'!

LAYING DOWN THE LAW

The king put forward three main demands. Firstly, that all future Church laws would have to receive the king's consent (in other words, be approved by him first). Secondly, a special royal commission would go through all the existing Church laws and decide which could or couldn't stay. Thirdly – and, boy, was this most importantly – that the Church in England got its power not from the Pope (or anyone else for that matter) but from the king. English bishops swore loyalty to the Pope in Rome. But shouldn't they be swearing loyalty to *him*? Henry reasoned.

A NEW WIFE

Although matters with the Church were still not sorted, Henry 'divorced' Catherine of Aragon and married the Marquess of Pembroke on 25 January 1533, in secret. The Marquess of *Who*? Oh sorry, didn't I tell you? Anne Boleyn had been getting so fed up waiting around to see whether she and Henry would ever get married, that Henry decided he'd better give her £1,000 a year and an important title. So in 1532, she became Marquess of Pembroke. The reason why they got married the following January was that Anne was pregnant . . . and, if the baby turned out to be a boy, Henry didn't want to run the risk of him being illegitimate.

This isn't how I imagined my wedding day would be!

Shhh! Keep your voice down! This is a secret ceremony.

AN AMAZING RESULT!

With a new (not-so-secret) secret wife and a baby on the way, Henry had to sort out 'the King's Great Matter' – as the business with the Church had become known – before the baby was born. Luck was on his side. The Archbishop of Canterbury died and the Pope's choice of new archbishop was none other than Henry's friend and adviser Thomas

Cranmer. On 23 May 1533, he agreed with Henry that his marriage to Catherine had been 'unlawful' because she'd been married to Henry's (now dead) brother first. In fact, in the eyes of the Church, they had never been married at all. This was the selfsame argument Wolsey had first put forward way, way back on page 30! Archbishop Cranmer then declared that the marriage between Henry and Anne Boleyn was legal and good.

CROWNING THE NEW QUEEN

Soon after, on a glorious summer's day, Anne Boleyn was crowned Queen of England. The streets were filled with people – of course they were; it was a public holiday with free drink – but very few of them threw their hats in the air or cheered. The truth be told, some even 'boo'-ed and shouted, 'Long live Queen Catherine!' Thomas More actually stayed at home.

A BASE FOR ROYAL POWER

Now that Cranmer had made it possible for Henry to remarry, it was down to Cromwell to give Henry absolute power over the Church and other matters. There followed a whole batch of parliamentary acts with such weird and wonderful names as *The Act of First Fruits and Tenths* and *The Act in Absolute Restraint of Annates,* but two of the most important ones were *The Treason Act* and *The Act of Succession*. The Act of Treason made it treason – punishable by death – to say that the king was a heretic. In other words, whatever Henry said about the Church was OK. In effect, he was now head of the Church in England.

THE ACT OF SUCCESSION

This dealt with the rather tricky subject of Henry's children. Now that his marriage to Catherine of Aragon had been declared not-a-marriage-after-all, their daughter Mary was officially declared illegitimate, as was Henry's son, Henry Fitzroy. She had no claim to the throne of England. Any children Henry and Anne Boleyn had would be heirs to the English crown.

BOUNCING BABY BESS

Much to Henry's disappointment, Anne Boleyn's baby turned out to be a girl. Born on 7 September 1533, they christened her 'Elizabeth', but little did anyone realize that she'd one day grow up to become queen. All Henry could think about back then was a legitimate son and heir.

ANOTHER TROUBLESOME LIZ

Another Elizabeth, this time Elizabeth Barton, was playing a very dangerous game. Known as the Holy Maid of Kent, she'd spoken out against Henry's plans to divorce Catherine in the past. Now she was saying that, having married Anne Boleyn, Henry would die a 'villain's death' in less than a month. A number of people believed Elizabeth Barton for two reasons: firstly, she had been miraculously cured of an incurable disease years before. Secondly, because she carried a golden letter sent down from heaven supporting her claims . . . at least her followers thought that was the case. (It does seem a little unlikely to me, though!) Henry wanted her executed but, for fear of upsetting her ever-growing following, he simply had her put in prison . . . and then hanged on 12 April 1534 when most people had forgotten about her.

THOMAS LOSES FAVOUR

Although for Catherine and against Henry's marriage to Anne Boleyn, Thomas More was careful not to side with the Holy Maid of Kent. He described her as a 'wicked woman' . . . but he too would soon end up dead. Henry's policy was along the lines of 'if you aren't with me you're against me' and More was being too wishy-washy. He just couldn't bring himself to swear to Henry's authority over the Church in England, so he ended up a prisoner in the Tower of London.

UNDER SENTENCE OF DEATH

When, in 1535, the Constable of the Tower, Sir William Kingston, heard that Thomas More was to be executed, he burst into tears. More told him to 'be of good cheer' and assured him that they'd all meet up again in heaven one day and 'be merry for ever and ever'. Henry had originally planned to have him horribly tortured before being executed, but he changed his mind. When Thomas More learnt of this, he made some joke about Henry being *so* merciful! He was then taken to the scaffold at Tyburn.

THE BEARD IS INNOCENT!

Thomas More had grown a long white beard whilst he was a prisoner in the Tower. Now he was resting his head on the executioner's block at Tyburn, he was careful to lift it free from his neck so that it trailed down the front of the block. Why? Because, as Thomas More himself declared, his beard 'had never committed treason'. Now it wouldn't get the chop when his neck did. He'd saved his beard's life!

WIFE NUMBER THREE PLEASE

Less than a year after Thomas More's bearded head was separated from his body, so was Anne Boleyn's beard-free head from hers. Not only had she 'failed' to give Henry the son he so badly wanted, but he'd also set his heart on a lady-in-waiting called Jane Seymour, and he didn't have to worry or give two figs about what the Church thought any more! After Anne was found guilty of seeing other men behind the king's back (which were probably completely made-up charges), she was executed on 19 May 1536. A razor-sharp sword was used instead of the more usual axe. How considerate. She was the second of Henry's wives to die that year. His first, Catherine of Aragon, had died on 8 January, of natural causes.

'NO GREAT BEAUTY'

Unlike Anne, who'd encouraged the king's advances, Jane Seymour was described as being 'full of goodness' and an honest, straightforward lady. In fact, she even returned his letters unopened, refused gifts and wouldn't see him in private – all things which ended up making Henry chase after her even harder. The moment Henry heard that Anne had been executed, he visited Jane Seymour and they became engaged. By the end of the month (May 1536) they were married. Now Anne's daughter, Elizabeth, was officially illegitimate along with his first wife's daughter, Mary!

NAMING HIS HEIR

Henry wasn't getting any younger and, with all his accidents and ill health (see page 33), he was probably beginning to suspect that he might die before he had a son and heir. There was a clause in the Act of Succession which said that he could name his own heir to the throne if he didn't have a son by his latest wife (in this case Jane). He probably planned to appoint his illegitimate son Henry Fitzroy, Duke of Richmond, but, sadly for the king, the duke died. Henry had him buried in secret. Now Henry began to think the unthinkable . . . what if he made one of his daughters – a WOMAN – his heir?

BACK IN COURT

After being shunned, Henry's elder daughter Mary suddenly found herself back in favour. She was allowed back in court and, along with her half-sister, Elizabeth, was made welcome by Jane Seymour who became a kind stepmother to them both. Mary, however, remained a Roman Catholic like her mother Catherine before her.

DISSOLUTION OF THE MONASTERIES

Apart from being big and bearded, having six wives and having people's heads chopped off, Henry VIII is probably best known for the dissolution of the monasteries. This may sound more dull than the other things that I've just mentioned, but it had an enormous effect on England and helped raise HUGE AMOUNTS OF CASH for the king.

THE *VALOR ECCLESIASTICUS*

Way, way, way back in 1086 – which was still way (singular) back in Henry's time – the then King of England, William the Conqueror, ordered the compiling of the Domesday Book. This listed the property and land ownership of England. (You can read about it in the super-fantastic *GET A LIFE! William the Conqueror*.) Now that Henry was the head of the Church in England, he wanted a similar kind of document listing all the *Church's* property and lands. It was drawn up by Thomas Cromwell in 1535 and was called *Valor Ecclesiasticus*.

A TREASURE TROVE

Jam-packed with detail, the report must have made mouth-watering reading for the cash-strapped king. All that land, those buildings and the treasures within those buildings now belonged to him . . . and what Henry needed most was M-O-N-E-Y. After all those parties when he'd first come to the throne and all the money spent on the army and navy and wars since then, here was a new, rich source of income. But what to do?

THE DISSOLUTION SOLUTION

I'll tell you what he did. He dissolved the monasteries – not in a giant vat of acid, but the result was pretty much the same. He threw out the monks, seized anything of value and let the buildings fall into disrepair. (They became a very useful source of building materials for new buildings and even farm walls. Why pay for stones when you could nip down the road and pinch them from an abandoned abbey or monastery?) Henry had done a great job in making the Church out to be the 'bad guy' so there wasn't much opposition. He'd start with the smaller monasteries and work up!

THE NAME'S BOND, VAGABOND

The countryside in Henry's day (and night) was pretty nasty. It wasn't all blue skies and pretty trees rustling in the gentle breeze. Most people were farmers or farmhands because you needed to grow food in order to have something to eat. The rich had huge farms. The poor farmed the common land that was for everyone ... The trouble was, the greedier the rich became, the more common land they fenced off for themselves, until there wasn't enough to go around. This left landless men roaming the countryside trying to find work, often stealing to stay alive. The rich saw them as landless louts and called them 'vagabonds'. To add to their number, there were now the hundreds of homeless monks left wandering about with nothing to do. So if you didn't run into a vagabond, you might well have met a monk.

TROUBLE UP NORTH

Trouble was brewing up in the north of England. There, people showed more loyalty to their lords and masters than to their king. Although the north was important because it was on the border with those wild and woolly Scots, Henry had never even been there. It was wild countryside and he'd heard that northerners were pretty wild too! Then, when Henry was enjoying rich festivities with Jane Seymour (Wife Number Three), at least partly paid for by those dissolved monasteries, there was a rebellion.

THE PILGRIMAGE OF GRACE

When Catherine of Aragon had still been queen, three powerful lords from the north – Thomas Dacre, Thomas Darcy and John Hussey – had plotted on her side and against the king. Now Catherine was out of the picture, they just plotted against the king in general! The closing of the monasteries was the last straw. A riot broke out in Lincolnshire on 1 October 1536 and spread, in pockets, across the country, but a much more serious uprising took place in York on 8 October. It was led by a one-eyed lawyer man named Robert Aske, who claimed that his group of followers were on a pilgrimage.

MAKING DEMANDS!

Aske and his 'Pilgrims' were a 40,000-strong army with four main aims: Henry and Catherine of Aragon's daughter, Mary, should no longer be seen as illegitimate, the Pope should be accepted as the head of the Church in England and, thirdly, the Church should be given all its powers and

51

property back. They even took it on themselves to reopen some of the local monasteries! The fourth aim was not a religious one. The Pilgrims wanted a proper parliament, one which represented the people and didn't simply agree to whatever the king wanted.

A MAN OF HONOUR

Henry's army was in such a pathetic state after years of fighting, that Aske's Pilgrim army could probably have marched into London and seized control. But Aske was an honourable man and he accepted Henry as his king (and a nice satin jacket as a present). Henry brought a promise of a parliament, and that none of his Pilgrims would be punished if they went to their homes, Aske agreed.

It's not a bribe, honestly... and you don't need to dry-clean it, whatever it says on the label.

A TURN FOR THE WORSE

Another rebel, this time a man called Bigod, whipped up support and, in February 1537, tried to take control of Hull and Scarborough. Unlike Aske and his Pilgrims of

Grace, he had always been *against* the Pope . . . but after he was defeated and his supporters hanged on the king's orders (including the monks who had reoccupied their monastery in Sawley), Henry used it as an excuse to go back on his word and have Aske hanged too.

DAZZLING PALACES

To go with Hampton Court palace (formerly Cardinal Wolsey's home), Whitehall (once the palace of the Archbishop of York), Greenwich (where he was born), Bridewell, St James's, Eltham and Windsor – this is getting to be a long list, huh? – Henry used some of his new-found wealth to build Nonsuch. It was so big and so grand that he had a village – including its church – knocked down to make way for it! And where is it now? Nonsuch? No such place, I'm afraid. It's all gone.

A ROYAL PRINCE

Riches or no riches, what Henry wanted most was a baby boy – a son and heir who would become king after him and carry on the Tudor name – and, on 12 October 1537, that's what he got. Jane Seymour gave birth to little Edward at Hampton Court, but it was to kill her. Twelve feverish days after the joyous event, she died. Thrilled to have a prince at last, Henry was equally horrified by his queen's death. She lay in state for three weeks before being buried in St George's Chapel, Windsor, in great pomp and ceremony.

She was the only of Henry's six wives ever to receive such an honour.

NEW TROUBLE

Pope Clement VII had died in 1535. His successor, Paul III, had been pushed too far. On 17 December 1538, he issued a bull (an official declaration) stating that, although he'd excommunicated Henry from the Roman Catholic Church in an earlier bull (back in '35), he hadn't made it Church law, in the hope that Henry might see the error of his ways, repent and come back to the Church . . . Instead, Henry had done things such as digging up the bones of Saint Thomas à Becket, trying them for treason, then burning them and scattering the ashes! (He also used the 'dissolved' St Augustine's Abbey to keep deer in.) This meant WAR!

THE KINGS OF CHRISTENDOM!

Pope Paul now called upon all loyal Roman Catholics to rise up against Henry. He couldn't have the bull actually published in England itself, but he made sure that there were copies floating around in France, Scotland and Ireland so that some would filter through into Henry's kingdom soon enough. Now it was a matter of taking sides. The Pope wanted Emperor Charles (he of Holy Roman Empire and King of Spain fame) to end the war he was having with the Turks at the time, and to attack Henry instead. Charles suggested that the Pope try to get France to take action against Henry, since he was too busy. But he would try to suppress the Protestants in Germany who might otherwise fight on Henry's side. It was all getting jolly complicated!

CRAFTY CROMWELL

With Jane Seymour dead, Henry was single again. Cromwell reasoned, what better way to get a foreign power on England's side than to make one of their princesses Queen of England? Henry should have a foreign bride! Henry rather liked the idea because he thought there were plenty of pretty princesses to choose from. Having divorced his first wife and beheaded his second, the possible brides-to-be were probably less thrilled at the thought of it!

IN THE FRAME

In France, there wasn't only the king's daughter, Margaret, but also the Duke of Guise's daughter, Marie, to choose from. But King James V of Scotland had his eye on Marie and he married her instead. Meanwhile, our Henry turned his attention to Christina, Duchess of Milan. Milan was an important piece of territory wanted by both Emperor Charles and King Francis. If he married the duchess, he'd be in a powerful position. He had the famous painter Hans Holbein paint a portrait of Christina to bring back and show him, and he liked what he saw. But the marriage was not to be. Next, Holbein painted Marie (now Queen of Scotland)'s two sisters, Louise and Renée . . . but there were others to consider too.

BEAUTY PARADE!

With so many possible brides out there in Europe, Henry decided to hold a kind of beauty parade for the 'hopefuls' in English-owned Calais. He suggested that the Queen of France could be there too, to make sure everything was conducted properly. King Francis didn't like the idea for a variety of obvious reasons. Not only was it *not* the done thing to parade women like horses in a show ring, but Francis was in secret meetings with his old enemy Charles and didn't want (anti-Charles) Henry to ruin everything.

WIFE NUMBER FOUR

By now, Cromwell was getting desperate to find Henry a foreign bride before the king got fed up with the idea not working as planned ... and he, Cromwell, got the blame! He told Henry of the 'beautiful' Anne of Cleves. Another Holbein portrait was painted and brought over to Henry, and he agreed to marry her. When she came to England, Henry was horrified. In his opinion, Anne was nothing like her portrait. He called her the Flanders mare – 'Flanders' being where she came from, and a 'mare' being a horse! Very reluctantly indeed (because he couldn't afford to offend the powerful families involved) he married poor Anne.

AN AMICABLE ARRANGEMENT

Henry and Anne of Cleves just didn't really get along from the word go. So, by the following year, he'd managed to divorce her, throwing in two manor houses, their flashy contents, an annual allowance and the rather odd title of 'the king's beloved sister'. Anne's (genuine) brother had wanted her to go back home, but Anne had grown to like England. She stayed on good terms with Henry and those who ruled after him. Dying in 1557, she was buried in Westminster Abbey.

CROMWELL GETS THE CHOP

Things might have stayed smiles between Anne and the king (relieved to get her off his hands) but they didn't stay so fine-and-dandy for Cromwell. Life seemed sweet for him. Henry made Cromwell the Lord Chamberlain of the Household in April 1540 but less than two months later he was arrested in the middle of a meeting around the Council table and stripped of his honours. Why? He was not only blamed for 'tricking' Henry into a loveless marriage to the 'Flanders mare' but – in a royal court where everyone was out to get everyone else – also accused of treason. If you think none of this makes any sense, think how poor old Thomas Cromwell must have felt! He wrote a letter to his king ending 'mercy, mercy, mercy', but mercy he did not get. What he *did* get was his head chopped off.

What's this word say? Mary? Mucky? Oh, never mind...

HOWDY HOWARD!

Next, Henry swiftly married the beautiful Catherine Howard. Catherine had been Anne Boleyn's cousin. Because of this, she showed a great deal of interest in Anne and

Henry's daughter, Elizabeth. She even sat the princess at an important place at the wedding banquet. To begin with, Henry thought his new – and very young – bride to be his 'blushing rose without a thorn'. Hearing rumours that Catherine had many lovers (some of which were definitely true), he soon changed his mind on that score! He had her executed on 12 February 1542.

SCOTCHING THE SCOTS

Throughout these marital 'troubles', there had been unrest in Europe too. Now France and the Holy Roman Empire had fallen out with each other again, Henry thought this would be an excellent time for England to attack France (so long as the Scots – who were ruled by a Roman Catholic king – didn't get involved). Henry flooded the Scottish border with troops, then offered King James V of Scotland a treaty. James refused. The Scots far outnumbered the English forces, but became stuck in the marshes of Solway

Moss. Few were killed, but hundreds of Scots were taken prisoner. King James died soon after – supposedly of shame – and his daughter Mary became Queen of Scots. She was a week old, so not too good at foreign policy.

PROPOSALS TURNED SOUR

On 1 July 1543, it was agreed that a 'treaty of marriage' be made between Henry's son Prince Edward and the baby Queen Mary. This was like an official engagement that would also bring peace . . . and Scotland pretty much under England's control. Now Henry could send 5,000 troops across the Channel to prepare to fight France. With the Scottish problem apparently sorted out, Henry and Charles V united against the French again (surprise, surprise) and planned a massive attack on France in 1544. The Scots then abandoned all its agreements with England and said, 'We're still friends with France really'. The engagement was now OFF and the English spent ten bloody days in Scotland doing some very nasty things to teach them a lesson.

SIXTH AND FINAL WIFE

In the same month that his son Edward was promised the hand of Mary Queen of Scots, July 1543, Henry married for the sixth and final time. His wife was another Catherine: Catherine Parr. (In fact, her name was Catherine Latimer when Henry met her because she had been married twice and outlived both her husbands.) Catherine Parr was kind and caring to all three of her stepchildren. Edward loved her, ten-year-old Elizabeth was obviously very fond of her and even Mary was delighted at how she recognized and accepted her 'royal blood'. Queen Catherine even stood in for King Henry as regent for a bit, while he was over on the continent fighting the French.

A VICTORY OF SORTS

The French town of Boulogne was captured on 18 September 1544. By October, Henry was trying to negotiate peace with the French. So much of the money he'd gained from the dissolution of the monasteries had been spent – some say wasted – on war. His health was really failing him now. He never seemed to be able to shake off a fever, his ulcers were extremely painful and he was carried everywhere. To get his huge hulk upstairs required a winch. By the time he was 55, he'd pretty much given up walking altogether.

MEETING HIS MAKER

Tradition has it that Henry died speaking the name of his third wife, Jane Seymour – the only wife to bear him a son, however sickly. Whether this is true or not, it certainly is true that his last will and testament was to be buried beside Jane in the chapel at Windsor. Henry died at about two o'clock on the morning of Friday 28 January 1547 in St James's Palace. He was holding the hand of Thomas Cranmer, the archbishop who had been with him through thick and thin. He squeezed Cranmer's hand as a sign that he put his trust in Christ. His reign of over thirty-seven years was at an end.

WHAT NEXT?

As you might expect, Henry's son Edward became king after Henry but ill health meant that his reign was a short one. Both of Henry's daughters were to become queen in turn too, but not before the nine-day (yes N-I-N-E D-A-Y) rule of someone called Lady Jane Grey. Roman Catholic Mary had a short but bloody reign whereas Elizabeth's was long and glorious . . . but that's another story, and you can read all about it in *Shortcuts: Elizabeth I*.

TIMELINE

At home and abroad

1491	Henry is born at Greenwich Palace.
1492	*Columbus almost 'discovers' America, but thinks it's China.*
1495-97	*Leonardo da Vinci paints 'The Last Supper'.*
1509	Henry marries Catherine of Aragon. Becomes King of England.
1512	*Michelangelo finishes painting the ceiling of the Sistine Chapel.*
1516	Birth of 'Bloody' Mary.
1519	Birth of Henry's illegitimate son, Henry Fitzroy.
1520	The Field of the Cloth of Gold.
1530	Cardinal Thomas Wolsey dies (before he can get the chop).
1533	Henry secretly marries Anne Boleyn. Archbishop Thomas Cranmer divorces Henry from Catherine. *The Spanish conquer the Inca Empire in Peru.* Princess (later Queen) Elizabeth is born.
1535	Thomas More executed.
1536	Catherine of Aragon dies (of natural causes). Anne Boleyn executed. Dissolution of the smaller monasteries. Henry marries Jane Seymour.
1537	Pilgrimage of Grace rebellion.

	Dissolution of the larger monasteries begins.
	Birth of Prince Edward.
	Jane Seymour dies.
1538	Thomas à Becket's tomb destroyed at Canterbury.
	Pope excommunicates Henry.
	First flintlock weapons used.
1540	Henry marries Anne of Cleves in January . . . and divorces her in July.
	Thomas Cromwell executed.
	Henry marries Catherine Howard.
1542	Catherine Howard executed.
1543	Henry marries Catherine Parr.
1545	The *Mary Rose* sinks.
1547	Henry dies.